# THE MAYAN POEMS
## James Schevill

*Cover painting, monotype and drawings
by Nathan Oliveira*

COPPER BEECH PRESS 1978

Acknowledgments to *New and Experimental Literature,*
edited by James P. White, and *Poetry Now.*
The story in *Priest to Jaguar* is taken from "A Document
Concerning Apotheosis" by David Jauss, *Puerto Del Sol,*
Summer 1976.

ISBN: 0-914278-16-9

Painting, Monotypes and Drawings
by Nathan Oliveira:
  Cover: Standing Figure, Oil, 1973
  Section I: Site VI, Monotype, 1975
  Section II: Fetish Drawing, 1976
  Section III: Site VII, Monotype, 1975
  Section IV: Fetish Drawing, 1976

This book was made possible by grant from the National
Endowment for the Arts in Washington, D.C., a Federal
agency.

*To Margot*

## MEXICAN FLOWER ARRANGEMENT

In a narrow water glass
on the porch overlooking the sea
my wife has settled
a thickstemmed red carnation
and a pale, pink hibiscus
its petals and delicate white veins
flaring out in the ocean breeze,
the little yellow pollinating dots
on its long pistil stem
a singular flagpole of color
    for a common waterglass.

As the poet, Pellicer, says,
flowers and death are the Mexican dreams.
To these I add the waterglass
and the hands of feminine love
that arranged the flowers
permitting the fragile hibiscus
to flutter against blue sky
and relentless spindrift waves —
If I were a painter I would paint
this stilllife with the naked arms
of the woman arranging the flowers
    for love against time.

# ONE

# VISION OF A MAYAN LORD

Horror of empty space . . .
    or vision of filled space . . .

From head to foot a portrait of detailed power
Monumental headdress as tall as himself
to command the sky,
    mask of the sun god carved in wood
on top swirl masses
        of bright green Quetzal feathers . . .

Skull flattened from birth into a narrow peak
    for the sake of beauty,
long hair braided with decorative ornaments,
face tattooed with intricate, dense patterns,
nose remodeled with putty to hook
into a half-moon curve of sensuous sculpture,
teeth filed and inlaid with jade,
perforated ears gradually enlarged
to hold the weight of enormous ornaments
    large as turkey eggs . . .

Eye purposely crossed like Japanese Kabuki actors
striking a Mie to spontaneous applause,
nose septum pierced to dangle jade bars . . .

Vanity of "suffocating ritual"
    or force of ritual presence . . .

Breechclout embroidered with brilliant colors
under it "the transmogrified penis"
    cut and flared like tassels of corn . . .

Over the breechclout a rich, anklelength skirt
woven by skilled weavers to command light,
belted with rows of small human heads,
affixed to the skirt a sacred jaguar skin . . .

To walk and gesture with jade glittering light,
jade rings on fingers and toes,
    bracelets of gold circling wrists, ankles . . .

"Artificial presence"
    or symbolic dream of life . . .


In one hand the authority scepter,
in the other a shield painted with the Sun God.
As he walks to his ceremonial place
not an inch of the naked man is visible . . .

Today we dream of the naked man,
    the true self,
truth as reality's bare details,
but the real shines in the dark,
    reality as style.
We seek again the mystery of ritual,
watch amazed as ritual fills space,
    obscures naked reality . . .

Only visions of Mayan Lords remain,
a few artifacts, jade ornaments in museums . . .

    Ritual is a haunting death
        or dream of birth
    Ritual is the terror in time
        we possess to conquer fear
    Ritual is the mastery of sentiment
        that the ugly may become beautiful
    Ritual is the abandonment of loneliness
        to enter the community of man
    Ritual is a mirror to see ourselves
        and journey forever into the soul
    Ritual is the music we make
        to accompany sacred silence

Ritual is the laughter that sings
  to release the comedy of appearance
Ritual is the death we celebrate
  to honor time's changing age
Ritual is the union of love
  flaring with sun into darkness
Ritual is the long breath we take in
  to breathe out in empty time
Ritual is the only resurrection
  flesh reborn in gestures of sun and moon

# THE MYSTERY OF THE MAYAN GLYPHS

Language . . . Does a Priest really desire to communicate?
His power lies in the lessons of God he has learned . . .
To create spectacular images of resurrected grace.
For this sophistication can he afford simplicity?
Yet he must bow to the warriors, the statesmen,
though his power surges from prediction, prophesy.
He must create signs that are mere pictures of things,
Enter a child's game of concrete poems, knowing
Real concrete poems require strange visual dimensions.

He creates bars and dots for numbers. These can be read
By any foreigner from tribes of different languages.
They are meant to assure an aristocratic eternity:
    This Jaguar-Prince, his name lost in time,
     Ruled during the Eighth Century, the Dark Ages in Europe.
    Dead power stands recorded subtly in lost time.

Such glyphs are not enough. To conceive of Zero
As a seashell is a lovely wedding of sound and vision
But only a start. Priests must startle time
With mysterious inscriptions. Priests must teach
Even if their students are only other priests.
Alphabets of communication must lead to Wonder.

Only the painful shape of syllables will teach;
Only the powerful sound of physical meaning will conquer.
Therefore Priests must become visual masters of time.
The transcendent mystery lies in enigmatic communications

That **require** interpretation, the Priest's rich function:
"To know is to speak my language,
    to fail is to speak your language.
I create my glyphs, I search for my natural gods."

 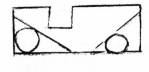

Wars rise from inferior syllables, false translations.
The problem of translation . . . Language is Death . . .
Language is also the resurrection of time . . .

# ON THE STYLE OF ASCENDING INDIAN PYRAMIDS

The Style of Cortes according to Bernal Diaz:

"When we arrived near the great temple and before we had climbed a single step, the great Montezuma sent six *papas* and two chieftains down from the top, where he was making his sacrifices, to escort our Captain; and as he climbed the steps, of which there were one hundred and fourteen, they tried to take him by the arms to help him up in the same way as they helped Montezuma, thinking he might be tired, but he would not let them near him."

*One hundred and fourteen steps to the gods,*
*To the sacrifices* — the pride and military caution
Of Cortes — stride upward in majestic solitude,
His horse of grandeur pawing at the pyramid's base,
Conqueror climbing to the sacrificial stone
Where a victim's heart ripped out by a jade knife
Pulsed glittering red in wind and hard blue sky . . .
Today I sit watching new styles of tourist ascent
To ruined temples on reconstructed pyramids:
A blond American dances up disdainfully
Delighting in the arrogance of youthful prancing.
A priest pauses, meditating on the horror in the sky
Before Christians slaughtered with sword and cannon.
Extending his arms, fat stomach, to the burning sun,
A Mexican runs up, laughing, stops in defeat
After twenty difficult steps, waves in resignation
To his grinning family below, plods slowly upward
Pushing the weight above him, memories of sacrificial
    time.
A crippled German crawls, measures with agonized
    precision.
Clinging to the rope an American housewife searches
    high

For her lost youth where a year ago a tourist fell to her
    death . . .

At 53 I climb or do not climb against my nearsighted
    vertigo
In search of legends, myths fading lost in time,
The sight of a jaguar with green jade eyes glistening
Through dark interior rooms; an immense funeral slab
Over the ravaged bones of lost Emperor or Poet-Priest.
I hope for my soul to fly through solitary space,
To realize through blinding sweat of fatigue
The communal mystery of man's hope, his war
Against implacable stone, his lust to create
Mountains, monumental pyramids of desire
That leave only questionmarks for questing time.

# MEXICAN WOMAN ON THE BALL COURT AT CHICHEN IZA

Running, jumping up the wall,
      grasping a stone fervently,
She leaps into the air,
      throws her rock at the tiny hole
Through which ancient players
      tossed their balls to win.
Failure. The rock bangs,
      slides off the stone rim.
Laughing, determined,
      she picks up another rock . . .
    (She runs backward into the past of games,
     Warriors clash in the ball game, lose, are sacrificed,
     Athletes preen in jewelry, feathered headdress,
     Often with scars on faces to indicate daring,
     Hachas to strike the ball attached to rigid waist-yokes)
She arches her hips as if placing her hacha in dream,
      runs, leaps again, Victory!
Her rock sails through, she jumps into her man's arms
      crying in triumph
Knowing a woman seldom wins in Mexico
      where all games are male:

*Octavio Paz:* "It is interesting that the image of the
*mala mujer* — the 'bad woman' — is almost always
accompanied by the idea of aggressive activity. She is
not passive like 'the self-denying mother,' 'the waiting
sweetheart,' the hermetic idol: she comes and goes,
she looks for men and then leaves them. Her extreme
mobility . . . renders her invulnerable."

*Her extreme mobility renders her invulnerable . . .*

The woman's sudden joyful leap
      triumphs in this ancient male game.
She is running through the 1970s
      in search of her future.

Yet she is not a *mala mujer*.
      Her aggression against her man
Warns of the open, free
      women's world that conceives men.
Winning is never for men alone
      as long as a woman waits.

# THE CENOTE AT CHICHEN ITZA

In a flat land where there is no metal
Vultures glide over us on wings of steel.
A huge iguana coils flat against a tree.
Gingerly we peek into the round cylinder
Of the Cenote . . . *No arroje Piedras al Cenote* –
Do not throw rocks into the well . . .
That silence is eighty meters deep . . .

Instead they threw sacrificial offerings,
Drugged victims to propitiate the gods,
Medallions of gold beautifully carved
(Dredged up by an early American consul) . . .
Reverently they threw in the victims
As if throwing them into eternal life.
Romantically the explorer, Halliburton,
Threw himself in twice, feet first, headfirst,
And received from the fall two headaches.

The well is quiet. Its surface coils with ooze
As though it conceals too many wonders
For which *sacrifice* is only a surface sensation.
Some scholars speak of "natural connections"
Rather than sacrifice. No, I am American
Taught language such as *wasting the enemy*.
Sacrifice to appease natural gods is not
In my military, my civilian vocabulary.
As I stare down at the stark-white limestone walls,
An American lady asks her Panama-hatted guide:
"Is it still *good* water?" He grins back,
"You see it is *still good* water, Madame."
My brain foams with clashing tones of *good*.

# THE FAILURE OF IMAGES AT CHICHEN ITZA

In a stone landscape
I take a stone siesta under a tree.
A guide approaches a neighbor stone.
Pointing his white cane at an image
The guide cackles to his tourist flock:
"Ladies and gentlemen, tell me
Is not this image of a dog
Very like Pluto in your comic strips?"
Gaping at the glyph a tourist gasps
    "That's Pluto all right."

In my stone siesta
I dream images, metaphors, pictures
Firing our senses with illumination.
Jumping up I rush to joyous Pluto.
A stunned lean dog stalks a dry landscape.
Beside the broken, discarded "Pluto" stone
Lies an empty Smirnoff vodka bottle.
    In dream we peer into
Time's ruins, a wilderness of perception,
Search desperately for images to save us
From destruction, striving to see
*Imago:* the shadow of history in time.

## TOURISTS AT PALENQUE

Curse tourists, condemned to be them
We travel in search of discovery —
Tourists as the ugly soul of ourselves,
The greedy, bumbling spirit we dislike,
Wishing to walk in foreign countries
With invisible mastery,
          bell-tongued explorers,
From superior explorations, mapped directions,
With money we leave no recreation to chance.
At the Temple of the Count I pause beneath a
Perpendicular Mexican who cries down, *"Hay nada."*
Despite his *nothing* I climb to see where
Count von Waldeck lived in 1832.
In tight-fitting jeans, dark glasses,
A blonde guide lectures a group of German tourists:
*"Hier lebt Graf von Waldeck – and he grew very ill*
*Because the difficult climate did not agree with him."*
Sweating, slapping, they nod miserably, cameras click:
"The mosquitos must have drilled him with delight."
Behind me an American teenager pauses to reflect,
"They should still use these buildings for religion."
Waldeck, phoney aristocrat, you drew false
    dream-palaces
Of Palenque to sell in Paris to lovers of romantic art,
But you knew we admire lost gods,
          we don't have to worship them.
Living gods compel us to crucifixion and sacrifice.

# PALENQUE
## (1) The Modern Town

Sitting on a black-red tiled porch
    of the sagging new hotel,
I stare at hills covered with jungle and Mayan ruins.
Flocks of white egrets arrow across the green foliage.
Isolated in history the little town of Palenque
    stirs warily in cooling evening air.
A thickset, barefoot woman, her dark hair
    dangling like tangled tree-roots
Walks up the dusty, rock-strewn road
    as though her bony feet were stone.

In the Zocalo American rebel kids
Search for deeper roots in mystical Mexico,
Listen to the juke box pour out memories
Of rock and Joan Baez
    at an old Viet Nam Peace Festival.
    (One song shrieks a mocking salute to the
    former California Governor — RONALD RAY-GUN.)

Four Mexicans stop to examine a building site
Where a worker has been making bricks all day
Slowly in hot sun, not thinking of ancient Mayans
Who built pyramids and tombs seven miles away.
    Meandering through the site, peering,
    Discussing gravely like philosophers,
    They lift bricks from the painfully made pile
    With resignation as if in this humid climate
    The world is a mountainous ascent
        that denies maintenance.

MAINTENANCE! Modern, anti-poetic word
    loved by pragmatic constructionists.

This new hotel is already crumbling,
        mold on the walls,
        electrical circuits ripped from sockets,
        equipment rotting in the empty swimming pool . . .

Slowly people flow out of their hot houses,
Sit in the square under shade trees to converse,
        watch the sun set, a remembered god.
Uncomfortably I stare at mystical Mexico
Where Americans joke at the failure of maintenance.

Over the square the Evening Star rises,
My wife sits on a bench with her tape recorder
        taping eager laughing children
        who sing folksongs happily into the machine.
I listen hard for the mystical god of maintenance,
His engineering eye that sparks his metal leaps . . .
Dead priests here listen to a different chant
Pounding slow natural rhythms of sun, moon, stars.
    Yet perhaps to listen for God is to maintain
    The soul, pure flow of water through this jungle,
    To search for and *maintain*
        (painful American word)
        the roots of history
    That we always kill in God's name for change.

## (2) In The Ruins

Which is more alive, town or ruins?
Somehow legendary ruins grow in time,
A town grows only with the ruins' fame.
   "Palenque was the Athens of the Mayan civilization,"
   the archaeologists preen as they measure the site.
False metaphors, we measure our shadows,
   the original, the ghost, dances away in time.
What can we say of curious pyramidal structures
Shining high in space with ornamental sculpture?
   *Corbusier:* "Architecture is a game — wise, correct
             and magnificent — forms playing under light."
A wise, correct game? Is all this architecture?
Do these death-tombs, ghosts of ceremonial dancers,
Lead only to lost time, vanity visions of eternal life?
   Time melts, fades, drips away in space,
   As space itself alters invisibly.
   Eternity has no sight, it changes angles of vision
   Like a fragile hummingbird pecking at sweet flowers.
If Spanish-Indian cultures teach us life's dream is real,
   The conquest of fantasy is also true,
   Time's fantasy in which we meditate.
   The ruins of Palenque are our ruins,
   Grace and beauty of natural environment,
   Architecture as sculpture,
       the purity of hand-shaped details.
   Impeccable aesthetics, ceremonial mastery,
   The community as blessing,
       but the ruins are dead.

History is time's enigmatic dream of ruins.
To measure history and conquer it is our aim,
History who gives us ruins
       to provoke our sense of wonder.

# TWO

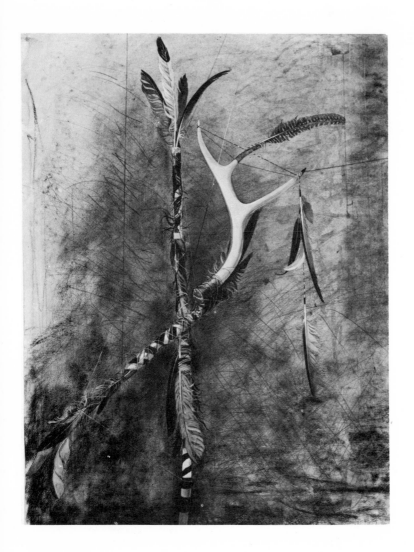

# THE LEGEND OF THE HOUSE OF THE DWARF AT UXMAL

Señor, how did that pyramid climb in the sky so perfectly round to honor the dead? Once an old woman lived there in a hut across from the Palace of the Governor. Of course these are Spanish names. The Indian names are lost in shadow. The old woman mourned because she had no children. One day in her sadness, praying to God, she took an egg and covered it with her black dress, warming the egg in sunlight, then guarding it in a corner of her heart.

For days she stared at it, warming it, praying to it, creating its new earth-life until one day the egg hatched, a baby was born, a baby of birds, animals, earth, yet seemingly shaped like a man. Pierced with a premonition of glory the old woman called the egg-baby, "My son." She hid it, guarded it, for a year taught it to walk, for a year taught it to talk until it sounded almost like a man. But after a year the baby stopped growing, remained in a curious Egg-Pygmy shape, half-man, half-child, yet the old woman praised this marvelous shape.

At night the old woman dreamt he would be a magician or a king. When she felt his destiny was assured she told him to go to the Governor's Palace, challenge him to a test of power. "He's only a Governor," she smiled, "a man of normal size. You're my son, an Egg-Pygmy, my magician of nature." "Go to sleep my little Egg-Pygmy," she soothed him at night. "Go to sleep and dream of your victorious walk to the Governor's Palace. Go to sleep and in the vision of your dream-walk you will see the triumph of the Egg-Pygmy."

In the night, as if jolted by an earthquake, the Egg-Pygmy woke with his head splitting to find with horror that a building was growing from his head. The dream-vision was becoming visionary reality. Suddenly at the rooster's crow of dawn the building turned into a flying machine shaped like a jaguar, hurtled the Egg-Pygmy over to the Governor's Palace and seated him on the Governor's Jaguar Throne under the silver crucifix.

"How did I get here, Mother?" cried the Egg-Pygmy, as he looked down from the throne at the tall Governor and his enormous soldiers. "Fly me back home!" "Nonsense," cried the old woman, "You flew over there in your own dream. You'll see what smallness does to his power."

So in his midget voice the Egg-Pygmy issued a challenge of smallness against largeness. Smiling his assent the Governor pointed to a stone weighing seventy-five pounds and told the Egg-Pygmy to lift it. Staring at this stone heavier than himself the Egg-Pygmy began to weep, scuttled down from the throne, scuttled across the barren desert to his mother's hut, moaning "Failure! Failure! That stone's as big as a mountain."

"You scuttle right back," scolded the mother, "You challenge the Governor to lift the stone first, then you'll have the dream strength to lift it too. And don't scuttle back.. Stick to your flying jaguar. If you lose your vision you'll get so small you'll wither away."

Alarmed at this possibility the Egg-Pygmy flew back to the Governor's Palace, caught him eating complacently with his family, and challenged him to another weightlifting contest. Amused and eager to entertain his family the Governor lifted the seventy-five pound stone with one hand and threw it contemptuously to the Egg-Pygmy. Staggering the Egg-Pygmy caught it and lifted it high in the air. Only then did he notice that he caught it and lifted it with his left hand. "It's a trick," cried the Governor. "Bring heavier stones!" The guards ran for heavier stones and set them up in a row.

As the Governor lifted each stone he shouted out in triumph, "I am the champion weightlifter." But the Egg-Pygmy's confidence grew as he discovered he could lift the stones with his left hand. At last the Governor's strength was exhausted and he shouted angrily at the Egg-Pygmy: "Build me a house taller and greater than this palace. I'll give you one night to build such a house, or I'll put you to death." Faced with this impossible task tears of frustration filled the Egg-Pygmy's eyes and he forgot his flying jaguar vision. He scuttled back again to his mother's hut as the Governor's family cheered with relief.

"Mother," he cried from a pool of tears, "I'm no architect, no sculptor, no craftsman. How can I build such a great house to say nothing of constructing it in a single night?" "Have you forgotten your singular dream-vision?" she answered, annoyed. "A mother does not labor for nine months to create an Egg-Pygmy without the assistance of invisible gods. Must I always be the one who leads you into the land of visionary reality? Go to sleep and seek your dream-destiny. In dreams small worlds become powerful."

In the middle of the night, frightened awake, the Egg-Pygmy bolted up with a vision of an enormous club banging against his head, his skull shattered. "Mother, Mother," he shrieked for help. "The Devil is attacking me." "It's only your vision, my stupid little son," she laughed at him. "You forget the ancient mysteries. Can't you see it's an imaginary challenge, a combat for the honor of smallness. You must challenge the Governor to a headbeating competition with clubs."

Despite another splitting headache the Egg-Pygmy summoned his flying jaguar vision to fly back to the Governor's Palace. The confident Governor called all the city's great men to witness the combat in the sacred Palace square. His mother's final instructions rang in the Egg-Pygmy's mind. "Remember," she had said, "You must always strike the *second* blow. After the winter freezes the sun always triumphs. You must wait for the right timing to be victorious."

"But Mother," the Egg-Pygmy stuttered in protest, "How am I going to survive the Governor's *first* blow?" Gesticulating with his tiny hands he couldn't express his fears. He kept seeing himself trying to strike the *second* blow without a head which had disappeared beneath the

Governor's *first* blow. "Have you forgotten your visions of magical helmets, magical crowns?" his mother scolded him. "Put on this crown, my little Egg-Pygmy, and rejoice in your defense." And around his head she molded a special tortilla. She pressed the dough into little hard points, baked it, and on his head placed the tortilla crown. "How can this appetizing crown ward off anything?" the Egg-Pygmy cried in despair. "If the Governor doesn't knock off my head, his dogs will eat me alive." "Be sure you get in the *second* blow," was all his mother answered.

As the ritual hour came the square filled with people loyal to their Governor: "Death to the pygmy boaster! Down with the tiny eggshell! Smash in his absurd tortilla crown!" Despite straining his visionary ears the Egg-Pygmy could not hear one supporter for his cause. He began to wonder about the nature of honor. Inspired by the loyalty of his subjects the Governor confided his new strategy to his wife: "When that miserable Egg-Pygmy was *second* in the weightlifting contest, he gained invisible strength. For some reason, perhaps because you have prayed too much to the Virgin Mary and not enough to the ancient gods, there is a danger of smallness. However, it's nothing that we can't adjust. I won't let him go second again. I'll force him to go first. With my strong head and a proper helmet that absurd Egg-Pygmy will make a fool of himself. Then I'll strike his head into a pulp and throw the pieces of his ridiculous tortilla crown to my followers to eat."

Trumpets sounded, flags blazed for the ritual battle. Half-naked drummers slashed a tattoo of sound as the Governor and the Egg-Pygmy marched out to select their weapons from a pile of huge clubs. Cleverly the Governor's guardian spies caused the Egg-Pygmy to select a light, ineffective club, while the Governor picked a heavy, knobbed club that could knock down a fence post.

As they faced each other across the square and the count to action began — *one, two, three* — the Egg-Pygmy lost his head. He forgot his mother's counsel. Scuttling forward he struck the first blow. The Governor laughed and broke his club over the Egg-Pygmy's head. Furious that nothing happened the Governor ran to the club pile, selected another club, and broke it over the Egg-Pygmy's head. His head still intact, though another splitting headache possessed him, the Egg-Pygmy staggered back. Losing his sense of ritual fair play completely, the Governor rushed again to the club-pile, seized a third club, and smashed it against the Egg-Pygmy's tortilla crown. Suddenly the tortilla crown glistened like gold in the sunlight. The crowd gasped in wonder and fell back. A voice in the crowd cried out — some swear it was a female voice — "Give the Egg-Pygmy his *second* blow." Mechanically, unaware of what he was doing, the Egg-Pygmy felt a club pressed into his left hand which he lifted without effort. The Governor turned and ran to avoid the Egg-Pygmy hitting back. But alerted to the cause of honor which requires give-and-take, the menacing crowd turned on the Governor and forced him back to the square. The Egg-Pygmy shattered the Governor's head with one lefthanded stroke, the skull flying in fragments of red flame through the square, leaving little sacred scars on people in the crowd who would forever afterwards devote themselves to the Egg-Pygmy's cause.

"Hail to our New Governor!" cried all the great men, the religious and secular leaders. "Hail to the Egg-Pygmy, our Lord of Smallness!" Dazed and crying with joy, the Egg-Pygmy flew home secure in the new vision of his power to find his mother dead on the floor, fallen, as if crushed with a blow. To bury her the Egg-Pygmy commanded a circular pyramid to be built. "It shall be curved," he ordered, "to shine like a woman's body. Bury her deep in a secret chamber, cover her eyes with jade. Stuff her mouth with jade so that she cannot talk to Death, make Death too powerful. For if she talks that old woman will conquer even Death."

Still, Señor, sometimes at night the round pyramid moves. Water flows out as if someone were crying inside. They say deep in there an old woman sits, a serpent beside her. She sells precious water to the spirits of Death to give her an Egg-Pygmy for the serpent to eat. And one day the spirits of smallness will rise again to conquer the Great Lords who boast of their giant strength. Tomorrow, Señor, tomorrow when you dream your masculine fantasies in your sleep and realize that life is a dream, the round pyramid will shake, the river of fertile tears flow out. Scuttling into the sun in his animal shape, his bird shape, his earth shape, his tortilla crown gleaming like gold, will scurry the Egg-Pygmy, lefthanded, to do his mother's bidding.

# THREE

# TWO VISIONS

## (1) The Upside-Down God at Tulum

Pelicans sail over the crumbling "Upside-Down" God.
Offshore in steady wind the coral reef glistens,
   white foaming line against sinking sun.
Bottom up, he kicks at the sky, peers down
To descend, transform, laugh his pleasure
At these strange mortals who make images of him.
Some call him a "God of Diving" because his
Sinuous buttocks arch in the air like a diver.
   "Upside-Down" or "God of Diving,"
Honor gods who descend to grasp humanity.
Fear implacable gods ascending with frozen eyes
   who stare hungrily into time.

## (2) The White Roads at Cobá

White roads, white roads, dream trails in time.
At desolate Cobá more than sixteen white roads remain.
American, I know the function of roads,
To speed free into time, find the endless journey of joy.
Slowly at Cobá the Chicleros move through dense forest,
Guns slung over shoulders, searching for chicle trees
That produce the sweet gum beloved of city children;
Peering for trees they stride over lost white roads.
I speed down the modern white road to Cobá,
Bounce three kilometers over the ancient *Sacbe;*
Swearing, sweating, we leave the car and hike
The rest of the way into the ruins, sad fantasies
Of barefooted messengers running over these rocks with joy.
White roads are not for rooted people.
Rulers command rooted people to dwell in security.
Only runners, winged animals, race on white roads
That secret messages may fly through space.

What travels on white roads may buy or sell
But it searches not merely for commerce —
Man, the hunting, running animal, delivering
Poetic mysteries to invisible hunters,
Gods who fly over the white roads of time.

# MAYAN SONGS

## (1) Marriage Song

To marry dance around her tree.
Praise, look deep into her eyes.
If they shine as deep as the sea
Look at her lips, listen to her sighs.

If peace rises from her skin
Like dew from a dawning tree
She will have pride to win,
Grace for the family to see.

Marry the shadowy light.
Seek woman in the moon;
Touch her skin at midnight,
She'll give you the sun at noon.

## (2) Washing Song

Good clothes must be cleaned
That colors shine brightly.
Rinse with laughter,
    nothing must be stained.
To walk in dirt is to walk in danger.
Clothes must shine in the darkest room.
    Dirty clothes are for the wild stranger.

Live in the open, wash in the stream.
Hang out the colors of joy to dry.
Soon life must sleep,
    after death is a dream.
To walk in dirt is to walk in danger.
Clothes must shine in the darkest room.
    Dirty clothes are for the wild stranger.

### (3) Song of Age and Youth

Let grandparents play
With children
   every wedding day

Old and young sit in the sun
Age and youth together
Against time's
   wrinkled weather

When old and young meet
The gods laugh with pleasure
Time begins, flows on
   for death cannot measure

# MAYAN DEATH-WAILS

"They have a great and excessive fear of death . . . When death occurred they wept the day in silence and at night they wailed."

Bishop Landa

## (1)

Death is myself,
Life is our people.
Oh it is terrible to die.
Death is alone.
Wail at Death.

I die alone
Defiling my people.
Death is a private sin,
Leaving my village.
Wail at Death.

To the Gods
Health and Life —
From Death darkness
and long voyages . . .
Wail at Death.

## (2)

With a crocodile spine,
cruel cutting eyes,
he crouches like a tiger
to eat my flesh.

I pray to the Death God,
offer him sacrifice.
Hideous his face . . .
The ugly Gods
are the ones to fear,
the ones to placate,
killers of peace.

With a hammering touch
and a stony jaw,
he grinds my life
like an ear of corn.

I pray to the Death God,
offer him sacrifice.
Hideous his face.
The ugly Gods
are the ones to fear,
the ones to placate,
killers of life.

### (3)

Wrap me in my shroud.
Place jade in my mouth,
a few jade beads.
Death must be paid,
Death is a mercenary,
Death the costly voyage.

A fisherman, I give Death
my nets and harpoons;
A farmer, I give Death
the tools of my life;
A warrior, I give Death
my shield and lance;
A Chieftain, I give Death
my dog to guide me
to Death's dark abode.
How greedy is Death,
Death is a mercenary,
Death the costly voyage.

Wrap me in my shroud.
Spare nothing to ornament my grave,
let the gold there glitter,

the beautiful jade gleam.
Death must be paid,
Death is a mercenary,
Death the costly voyage.

### (4)

*Cumhau, Ah Puch, Cizin . . .*
how many the Death Gods,
how sinister the sound
of their crunching names.
Wail at Death.
*Cumhau, Ah Puch, Cizin . . .*

Oh I am afraid
to hunt for Paradise.
The voyage is long
and the Night Lords wait.
Wail at Death.
*Cumhau, Ah Puch, Cizin . . .*

Fill my grave with food
and something to drink,
or how will I live
in the World of Death?
Wail at Death.
*Cumhau, Ah Puch, Cizin . . .*

There, no food grows,
no fields lie open
fallow in sun.
Nothing grows there,
Wail at Death.
*Cumhau, Ah Puch, Cizin . . .*

Down through the layers
of the underworld I go

where the Lords of Night
rule in darkness.
Wail at Death.
   *Cumhau, Ah Puch, Cizin . . .*

How many the Death Gods,
how sinister the sound
of their crunching names.
Wail at Death.
   *Cumhau, Ah Puch, Cizin . . .*

# PRIEST TO JAGUAR:
## APOTHEOSIS IN GUATEMALA, 1550

### (1)

For twenty years I have lived disgraced,
Known as a man who has taken an Indian wife,
A defrocked priest from whom the cowl has fallen.
Children call my son "Son of the Devil."
The church will not admit him for baptism or learning.
He grows in the street like an animal.
I was the prefect apostolic of the Mercedarians,
Master of all religious instruction,
Trusted administrator of the sacraments,
Construction supervisor of the single-naved church
Within God's fortress of Santiago Atitlan.
The first quarter of my mission I witnessed the baptism
Of two thousand natives, in the second quarter three
    thousand.
As the sacred bells rang in my ears I knew
*The glory of God moves even through these savage
    people.*

### (2)

When our church shone white in the sun, the golden
    cross gleaming,
We began to instruct the Cakchiquel children in the
    catechism.
An Indian boy was drawing idly, not listening to Fray
    Zumarraga's lecture.
Angrily, robes flowing, I snatched the drawing from him.
Loudly I proclaimed, "We have an idle boy who is
    drawing."
In the drawing a woman stood on the horns of a crescent
    moon.
"Who is this woman?" I questioned the boy sternly.
"The Virgin Mother," he answered. Looking closer

I saw the woman was holding stalks of maize in her
  hands.
"Why don't you draw the Virgin crushing the serpent's
  head?"
I suggested gently. The boy stared at me with wonder.
"No one can crush the powerful head of Quetzalcoatl."
Startled, angry to hear the name of that pagan god
I seized the boy's elbow firmly, ushered him out of the
  church.

### (3)

Robed black against the hot sun I ordered the boy
To tell me about Quetzalcoatl. He stared at the earth
In defiant silence. I raised my hand to strike him.
Suddenly he spoke, afraid, a litany of praise.
"He created sky and earth, the four directions.
He told the wind gods to blow, the rain gods
To empty their dark clouds. He created the Obsidian
  Stone
And with his power the first man and woman."
Shouting at the boy my mind whirled dizzily:
"Have you not learned the evil serpent caused man's
  fall?"
The answer came in a voice beyond the boy's age:
"Quetzalcoatl is immortal like the bird, wise like the
  serpent."
The challenge was set. I claimed the boy for training.
In teaching him long hour after hour I often closed my
  eyes
And thought with pity, "Their God is a serpent."

### (4)

When I took the boy into the monastery house my
  brothers objected.
Their resentment grew. I planned an act of wonder to
  restore their faith.

One evening at my invitation issued through the boy's
     father
All of the Indian priests gathered watchfully in the
     church.
In the vestry I placed three Spanish priests of great
     strength
In case the deed I planned should cause an act of wrath.
Upon the altar I put a wooden cage covered with a sacred
     vestment.
Pulling off the vestment I disclosed to the Indian priests
A glowing Quetzal bird fluttering vainly in the cage.
With gloved, imperial hand I snatched out the bird
Feeling the same pulse of pride and fear as in my first
     Mass.
I felt God spoke through me and I called in His voice:
"I will show you the folly of your false worship."
With a stiletto I lanced the bird's heart on the altar.
An inner voice whispered, pounded, *"Now they will kill
     me,"*
I cried for protection from my strong-arm priests,
But looking down I saw the Indian priests falling in fear.

(5)

Secretly, two days later, the Indians vacated the fortress.
Alvarado's captains ordered the garrison to prepare for
     siege.
Four days of armed silence prevented the mood of
     prayer.
The next morning the Cakchiquels attacked the fortress.
Scaling the wall by ladder an Indian raised high
Alvarado's severed head. Despite our superior weapons
The Indians flourished like flies, their small insect bodies
Armed with knives, breast-plates, helmets smeared with
     blood.

Isolated in the vestry I watched with horror as the savages
Slit the stomach of our proconsul's pregnant wife.
"Hail, Mary, full of grace," I prayed, "the Lord is with
  thee."

### (6)

Kneeling, struggling to pray, when the savages entered
Blood-stained, I heard my ghost voice cry for mercy,
"I am your Brother. Do not kill me!" They led me away
Behind the head of Alvarado dancing on a pole,
I alone of sixty-four captured missionaries was not
  bound.
Dazed with life, hands free, ashamed, I was led
To the Indian priests in their bright feathered costumes.
An old man, his long nose hooked in a half-moon curve,
A golden chain of feathered birds around his neck,
Sentenced me to trial: "We must know if you are
God or Demon. We will learn if we must fall on our knees
Before you or offer your heart to Quetzalcoatl."
When I asked about my brother priests he proclaimed
*They will die.* All because I killed a Quetzal with a
  stiletto.

### (7)

During the journey to Sololá, spears prodded my side.
The Indian priests rode ahead on our captured horses.
I walked through the nightmare battlefield, saw my
  countrymen
Headless, scattered in grotesque shapes of death.
After the battleground we entered a dark forest
On the lake's western ridge. I could walk no further.
I fell to my knees, praying, suffering from guilt
Because I had not told my brothers of my failure to
  convert the boy.
On orders of the Indian priest I was tied, gagged,
  hooded,
Led by a halter like a horse through the forest.

## (8)

In my blind, hooded world I heard the sound of water
Hurtling over rocks. We were near the river Quicab.
Swaying dizzily we crossed the gorge on a rope bridge
And I created visions of myself as defiant suicide
Or falling victim until safely across, stumbling on,
I was only dragging captive. When stone doors scraped
In my ears we entered Sololá, their sacred city.
As my feet touched stone and I was ordered to ascend
I felt despair as I was climbing the Avenue of the Dead,
The sacrificial pyramid of Quetzalcoatl. At the summit
They cut off my clothes, I sensed the knife ready
To strike into my heart. I prayed to God and the Virgin
As my hood was cut away. Arms and legs open
To the four winds I stood, naked, staring down at a sea of
    faces.
*Do they know who I am?* Their cries of joy proved my
    identity.

## (9)

Priests tore me from my rigid stance, took me to the
    ceremonial chamber.
On the chamber's walls a feathered serpent rode the sun,
Bright quetzal birds ate human hearts, from his erect
    penis
A priest sowed a field with fertile seed. The chief priest
    spoke:
"For seven days and seven nights you will remain without
    food
In this chamber, guarded. Then the time of the feathered
    serpent,
The ceremony of apotheosis, will come and we will know
If you are white god or white demon." Cutting all light off
He fastened a jaguar hide over the chamber's doorway.
Naked I felt myself strong and prayed to God to die a
    martyr

Remembering with guilt my joyful stance to the four
   winds.
For four days my hunger grew. After seven days my
   parched mouth
Prepared me to live or die as the chief priest chose.

### (10)

The jaguar hide was torn away. I was led into the brilliant
   sun.
Covering my eyes I fell curling up in a womb-like trance.
Voices mocked me, "Are you hungry?" "Would you like
   a cool drink?"
My heart pounded *yes* though I felt my head shake *no.*
Then the chief priest spoke, a voice firm with pride
As the invisible wind proclaims its powerful design.
"He is ready. Give him the holy liquid. He is ready."
Bitter and thick the taste, but I drank all in my thirst.
The priest approached me, an obsidian dagger in his
   hand,
The green jade serpent crawling up the handle.
"He will kill me as I killed the quetzal," I thought,
But he put the dagger in my hand and began to instruct
   me
In the ritual I must perform. I was to cut my arms, legs,
Tongue, and genitals at sunrise and at sunset, then offer
My blood to Quetzalcoatl burning in a cup of copal gum.

### (11)

For the blood ritual I was led down into the pyramid's
   heart
Below ground, a journey to the underworld for blood
   sacrifice.
They placed me on a stone altar. Braziers burned around
   me
With the stench of smoking blood. How I made the cuts
I do not know, but I saw in the burning blood-light

The incisions. My mouth filled with blood from my
   tongue
And I spat it into a bowl. As the priest poured my blood
Into the brazier, it blazed up and I felt a sudden
   exultation.
What difference did it make, Christ or Quetzalcoatl?
My blood was burning into time, my flesh glorified by
   sacrifice.
I agonized: "This glory is not mine. It is the blood
   speaking."

### (12)

The priests must have drugged me for I fell asleep.
I dreamt of grace, the power of pity and atonement,
Though I could no longer think what I should atone for.
Day after day I continued to make the ritual cuts,
Watched my red blood poured into the braziers to burn.
Without concern for damnation I continued in my sin.
By the fourth day the bloodletting severely weakened
   me.
That night, after the ritual cuts, I refused the drug for
   sleep
Telling myself *I will die conscious of my own identity.*

### (13)

On the fifth day the priest began to tell me about
   Quetzalcoatl.
He spoke gently as if telling me a story to cure my illness.
In the beginning Quetzalcoatl created the Obsidian
   Stone
And then created Man, mixing the dough made out of
   maize
With blood from serpent and quetzal in homage to the
   Stone.
"Once before when Quetzalcoatl became man," the
   priest told me,

"His mother tore off his umbilical cord and hung it
From this temple door as a sign of his divine birth.
Then she threw herself down from the pyramid so that
Her designated son would promise to return again as
   God."
Listening I heard the god speak, his birdlike voice,
His serpent thought. That evening I tried to strike out
My life with one blow, but instead carved the incisions
And watched my blood flow. To urinate was to burn,
My tongue flamed like a coal in my swollen mouth,
I could not clench my fist for the pain in my arms.
I prayed not knowing whom to pray to, so I stopped.

### (14)

Waking to dream after five days of blood-burning,
I was given a staff carved with a snake and quetzal's
   wings.
Carried up into the light I was displayed again to the
   people.
As they cheered, my body began to swell with the sound
   of my new name.
They paraded me through the crowded square, the
   shouting populace,
Past my former brother missionaries whose cries for help
Floated softly past my ears. Restraining the pleasure in
   my power
I reassured myself: "Just before they reach the point of
   sacrifice
I will speak through my grace and order them to be
   saved."

### (15)

Ascending the pyramid to the sacred summit I was seated
On a carved throne behind the sacrificial altar.
In the inner ceremonial chamber glowed a huge fire.
Wearing a mask brightly covered with a serpent's snout
And a cloak feathered with a quetzal's gold and red
   plumage,

The Indian priest appeared holding his hands high,
His knuckles shining with the sharp claws of a jaguar.
He chanted my name and the chant echoed below from
the people.
Slowly the missionaries were led up the steep steps
Called the Path of the Dead. As the first approached my
throne
I knew his pale face, but could not remember his Spanish
name.
While I watched they stretched him out on the altar.
To purify him they took the worms and frogs of evil from
his mouth.
Then the priest plunged the obsidian knife into his heart.
All of the missionaries were killed while I watched on my
throne.
I asked to sleep away this horror, but the hearts still
pumping
For life were brought to me to celebrate my
transformation.
Without eating, I fainted, yet when I recovered
consciousness
My health, my superior strength, seemed again
transcendant.
I tried to imagine the food I had eaten was a familiar diet,
But slowly the horror of my apotheosis filled my mind.

### (16)

As a god I was not guarded and I planned my escape.
The Indian priest said only, "You are a fool if you think
You can escape your blood." I ordered a canoe to be
prepared
And the priest with his retinue watched me depart.
In the river's rapids I almost foundered before reaching
the lake.
In calm water I floated for a moment before I paddled
through

The drifting, heartless bodies of my fellow missionaries.
Their bloody chests yellow with pus gaped at the sun.
Caught in this sunlit nightmare I paddled desperately
Through a sea of bodies. The stench from corpses and my
soul was great.

### (17)

Arriving half-dead at Santiago Atitlan a new group of
missionaries
Who had just arrived carried me into the monastary
house.
They cared for me. When my health improved I feigned
illness.
The dream of hearts I could not cure. I could not confess
My sins or receive the Holy Eucharist. My Spanish
brothers
Began to look at me as if I were some curious foreigner
No longer tied to the masculine world of spiritual service.
I sought out a woman and paid her for the peace of her
body.
With the sun's force I pierced her, got her with child,
And lived then as an outcast, a leper to be avoided as
unclean.
For twenty years I have lived on, marked, unrepentant,
Dreaming at night of my jaguar claws, dreaming of Christ.
I am regarded as a *nadie*, a *nothing*, but I know a *nothing*
Lives suspended between two worlds, between two
gods,
Christ and Quetzalcoatl, and only a *nothing* can know
The power of both and, what I feel, the power of a
*nothing*.

# FOUR

# A ZINECANTAN VILLAGE ON EASTER FRIDAY

In glaring white man's mask,
Swinging from a rope over the church door,
    the Judas Dummy twists slowly;
Cowboy hat, jeans, polished riding boots,
Left hand caught in a gourd-like bag of maize,
This Judas will never seed good corn again,
    his traitorous hand
    sticks in the seed for eternity.

Underneath the Judas Dummy
The Zinecantans flow pinkly into church,
    their clothing blossoms
Like fragrant petals, a cluster of pink flowers
Harmonizing the color of village unity.
In the church pink unity settles in prayer.
    A carved, tortured Christ
    staggers under the altar cross.

The Indians dangle pink ribbons from Christ's neck
To celebrate his tormented passage through the world,
    pray to their own Sun, Moon, Fire Gods.
No white priest is visible in this Catholic church.
By the altar two men in white breechclouts
Over brown muscular legs move like dancers
    through a glittering
needle-sharp forest of candlelight.

They swoop, light more candles, place them high.
The flickering web grows so intricate, honey-combed,
    golden air flows thick as honey.
A flute wails its high, nasal, wooden phrase
Spasmodically, over and over, repetition as resurrection,
A pink and honey celebration of eternal sacrifice
    to turn the single ritual of candles
    into a communal offering of light.

Outside under the Judas Dummy village elders
Sit on benches, wise men, medicine men, shamans,
        drink in communion
To acknowledge tribesmen arriving for this crucifixion day.
Heads wrapped in white turbans summoning light,
The elders chat gravely, point to their sacred mountains
            where old gods still require sacrifice
            of chickens now instead of men.

Across the street in modern council chambers
A tribal leader hears problems, complaints,
        a daily line of grievances
While history continues under the Judas Dummy.
Timeless religion, daily politics flow together
On this Hebraic Foreigner's Day, the strange visitor
            who traveled to this village
            to share their pain, joy, their gods.

Behind the church in the village center
Proud tribesmen, multi-colored ribbons
            dangling from flat strawhats,
Exchange family news, eat in casual friendship
To renew blood communion. No one glances up
At the hanging Judas Dummy, white menace still
            swinging to seduce them into
            the luxury of industrial time.